MW00914877

This book belongs to

Made in the USA
Las Vegas, NV
06 November 2023

80337506R00056